Becoming a Wildflower

poetry + prose for courage

April Green

Also by April Green:

Bloom for Yourself
Bloom for Yourself II – Let go and grow

Wildflowers grow wherever the wind takes them; wherever the wind chooses to lay them down, they grow.

They don't look at their environment or the circumstances that brought them to where they are. They don't look at who is next to them, in front of them, or behind them.

They turn their faces to the light; and they grow.

('Bloom for Yourself II, Let go and grow'
by April Green)

Cover Artwork:
Xavier Esclusa Trias
www.twopots-design.com
xevi@twopots-design.com

ISBN–9781794418981

For my beautiful readers: in whatever part of the Universe you occupy, I am sending you these words, these flowers pressed to paper, in the hope that you will find the courage to keep stretching and growing beyond anything you ever imagined.

Becoming a Wildflower

Becoming a Wildflower

On days when I feel like giving up;
when dawn stretches out ahead of me
too wide, too long to face,
night still tight around my neck,

this is the prayer:

I don't know where I'm going.
I can't always see the path in front of me,
and even when I can,
I don't always recognise the person
I am,

but somewhere at the back of me,
in that delicate space between spine and air,
are the hands of the woman who survived
all the days that brought me here.

So, for her—I will rise.

April Green

Grace

She showed me
where the flowers were hidden
then she left me to bloom.

What the wildflowers teach us

She crouched down beside me, a flower pressed into her hand, white petals beneath her feet. I saw the future in her eyes, an ocean tugging me in—the way the moon tugs your bones when she's at her fullest, reminds you to look up.

I held the flower, a life in my hand: 'How can something so crushed still smell so sweet?'

'Remember, you don't have to stay the same.' She said. 'You bleed, you move, you spill life into everything you touch—that's what the wildflowers teach us.'

Then I watched her walk away, a vision of peonies and promises, as though watching her leave was watching myself arrive.

And I heard her whisper:

'Darling, whatever you do:
please try and transform the pain
into something very beautiful.'

Sometimes, people come along
to show you the parts of yourself
you didn't know existed.

And, when they leave—
you are altered:
you are braver, stronger
than ever before.

April Green

And maybe courage
isn't so impossible to find.

Maybe courage
is the tender touch of dusk upon my feet,
whispering:

       'rest awhile; try again tomorrow.'

The silence after rain:

> how quickly the sky pulls herself
> together.

April Green

The ceremony of healing

Slowly, deliberately,
I become a field of flowers
and
listen to the wild dawn
tearing night from her skin.

It is a gentle violence,
a breaking open:

life starting over again.

April Green

Surviving is hard:

It's okay to take your time
bringing yourself back to life,
honouring how far you have
come.

Cosmic order

The ocean has my wishes inside her, thrown like rain from a body of water, a body of light.

You can't teach a person what you know: you can't tell them that every prayer, every word unspoken, every feeling moving through your bones like a loose tongue, always returns with the wind and the tide.

So, love: surrender while you can, on knees wet with earth and the bruise of thunder, because nothing is random—it is wished for.

It is magic.

Fragile

One of the hardest things I have ever had to admit to myself was that during my most fragile years, I allowed others to treat me the way I treated myself.

(lack of self-worth stains everything the colour of itself.)

April Green

Becoming a Wildflower

I am grateful
to the ones who
misunderstood me, rejected me,
tried to dim my light—

for they led me back to myself.

April Green

Returning

And just like an injured bird, she remembered how to fly without depending on anything but the air to carry her.

When you are gentle
with yourself,
with your healing—

you come back to life.

And perhaps,
the most beautiful flowers
are the ones who allow the rain
to pass right through them.

April Green

Becoming a Wildflower

When I see them;
the broken,
holding something,
anything,
that will break them
some more;
there are things I want
to say, like:

how would the ocean turn pink
if the sky held onto the sun
like that?
How would the rain fall
and disguise
your silent tears?

I was once like you—
we weren't born
holding things;
we were holding nothing.

We were held.

We are still held.

(I pray that you one day find the courage to let go and
discover just how much you are held.)

April Green

Let it go
then see what kind of magic
returns in its place.

Because,
I promise that
what's for you
will never reach you
while you're clinging
to something else.

April Green

The quiet confidence
that comes from walking
away.

(and how your body raises you higher
with every step.)

Choices

I hope you understand that no-one can take away any part of who you are. It is your experiences that should be guiding you towards choosing the parts that no longer serve you, nothing else.

That's what makes living with yourself, as yourself, all the more beautiful—every choice is yours.

The world within

As a child,
I had needs that weren't always met.

Growing up,
I expected everyone and everything
to give me those needs.

As an adult,
I have discovered that I have
enough power inside me
to give myself everything
I need:

validation / nurture / unconditional love / respect /
expression / encouragement / belief / courage /
strength / grace / empowerment / freedom.

The beauty of pain

Believe me when I say that the storms in your life contain beautiful mosaics of learnings and wisdom that will lead you towards an incredible life.

But you must be brave enough to weather the pain of each storm. You must believe that you have the strength to rise from the aftermath more alive than ever before.

Expression needs no language

We all have a deep, inherent need to feel heard. Without judgement. Without apology—but from the very root of who we are—from the inside out.

But what do you do when you don't feel heard?

Listen to yourself. Listen to what your soul is drawing you towards. Express yourself without words. Do it in a way that says:

'I am here. This is the only voice I need.'

Always return to yourself

If ever you feel lost and alone, please learn the art of becoming so still that you reconnect with the magic of your soul.

You are never truly alone.

You are made of stars and love

Your reason for being
is not to explain yourself
for being.

Even if it sometimes feels
as though you're wrapped inside
your own little planet,
hurtling through outer space—

you still belong here.

(never apologise for your light.)

April Green

Reminder:

Don't forget:
you're the one
who has been there
for yourself
all along.

April Green

Return to love

You were made from love,
out of love, and beyond love—
beyond anything you can even comprehend—
and sometimes you will stay there.
sometimes you won't.
sometimes you will drop down to
the lowest energy that exists
and you will have to climb hard
to get back to love.
sometimes you will fight with the truth:
cling to lust, desire, addiction, obsession
and call it love.
sometimes you will hold on to comfort
and stay there for days, months, years,
even a lifetime
before you return to love.
sometimes you will give up completely
and that's a good thing. that's a good thing.
because, somewhere between climbing
and falling and fearing and loving
will you eventually work out that
surrendering
is the only way to control the movement,
the energy, the fire.

surrendering
is the only way to return to love.

April Green

Feel everything—
even if you're terrified,
(especially if you're terrified)
because I promise
that courage will rise
to the surface
when you need it the most.

April Green

The taste of another chance

It's a beautiful thing: to know that, every day, we get the chance to pull back the skin of the air, heavy with the bones of the past, the dust of a storm, and step into a new space surrounded by light we've never seen before.

You

You aren't less of a person because someone has rejected you.

Remember—not everyone is ready to meet you where you are because they're not yet ready to meet themselves where they are.

Be patient:

The ones who deserve you will always find a way to reach you, I promise.

Know when to walk away before you are hurt beyond repair

Learn to read the feeling you get when something isn't right. Take that feeling and hold it tight; trust that it's right. Don't wait until it fades in colour, turns to rose, because nothing will hurt you more than the result of ignoring that feeling.

I know. It's hard. And it may mean walking away. But you have to trust your heart. You have to trust your heart over anything else, because the heart energy doesn't lie.

The heart energy is the truth.

The only way to be free
of what could have been is
to start a new chapter,
create a new story.

If you have to leave someone:

Do it because you are both no longer
right for each other.

Do it because you both need to grow.

Don't you dare make the other person 'wrong' as a
way of justifying leaving them.

(you have the freedom to choose without feeling
any guilt.)

When the soul longs for something the hands can't reach

Some of us are born with a hole in our souls; eyes that wander towards anything that even slightly resembles the missing piece. We were whole once, I am certain. But when our star exploded into the cosmos, a tiny fragment split off into space, and we search for it in everything we touch. We lift mountains, and rivers, and skies; tear ourselves open, pull ourselves apart until, one day, we slow down, we stand still, we become who we are.

You see, creation blew the hole out of us in the first place; but living from the soul: creating a life, a purpose, a piece of art, fills it back in again.

Reminder:

You don't have to
make sense of it all.

You just have to know that,
in spite of it all,

you are stronger.

Note to self:

I am becoming
a master at sitting
quietly in the space
between
my emotions and
my reactions.

I will not be moved by
another person's pain.

My body is soft:
nothing will harden me
again.

April Green

Becoming a Wildflower

I will not tell
my daughter that
she can be anything
she wants.

I will tell her
to be herself;
and then anything
she wants
will float beautifully
towards her.

April Green

Running away takes you places you've been before

I used to think that running was the answer: run from the body, the face, the people, the problems. Fast, like the speed of light, and maybe the colours and borders will blend, and things will look different, feel better. But I kept reaching places I'd been before: same problem disguised as a different sunset.

And then I started to see that a thousand different sunsets will tell you the same thing—

you can't run from the root.

So I started to face the light. I started to reflect what the Earth was showing me; and the world came to me.

I was standing in the answer.

You have spent too long pretending you're okay

I know that you hurt sometimes. I know that you're afraid to talk about it for fear of disturbing it; afraid that if it moves, expands, rises like a sudden breath, you may sink to the ground and never return. I know that you're trying to keep it all inside until you forget, but it's hard to forget while it's there, and it's heavy, and it's hurting, so you're going to try and forget forgetting; but that's just going to make you numb, and numb is something you do not deserve to be. You deserve to feel the air brushing your skin, the sun kissing your face, kindness reaching out to you from another person's eyes. So, please believe me when I say there is another way; a better way:

Whatever you are feeling, someone else is feeling too. The world is full of people carrying too much pain and not feeling able to talk about it. But, if you could just try to whisper it, I promise that the sound of your voice, your words, will break something open inside. The pain will be released, and it will fall through the air like filtered light.

You will come back to life.

Just for today

And I know there are days when you count the hours and minutes until you can draw back the bed sheet and climb inside; hide from the world, be yourself, cry with yourself, talk with yourself.   Sometimes, I am certain I can hear us whispering the same words:

'Just for today, it's okay if I rest like a flower in the shade and start again tomorrow.'

April Green

The art of bravery

Remember—a brave person doesn't always know they are brave until they have no other option but to become fearless.

For the ones who are healing:

When you are healing—
set some boundaries.

Do not let them treat you
as you were.

Do not treat yourself
as you were.

You are stronger now.
You are healing.

Reinforce yourself with a boundary;
it is not a wall,
it is soft,
it is protecting you.

Because:

> You did not dig your soul
> out of the dark
> to hand it to someone else.

April Green

You don't have to fall apart:

It may not feel like it has,
but pain has a purpose;
heartbreak has a purpose.

So, break.
A thousand times
and more,
because breaking (open)
is part of growing:

> it allows the old life to be free
> and
> the new life to take its first breath.

One thing I know for sure:

When you stop looking for yourself
in the arms of others, or
in the reflection of all those shiny things
filled with nothing but false promises:

you will find your authentic self.

Love. Breathe. You belong here...

Remember the time when you didn't think you could carry on; when the sky fell in on you like an old memory and the stars floated further away?

> And here you are, still: wildflower turning towards light.

Never forget that there is endless grace in the place where you're standing. Never forget that you belong here—exactly where you were designed to be.

Don't complicate your journey by explaining your journey

Don't justify why you did a thing, or why you do a thing—you can put your heart in your mouth, give away your words, your kisses, your secrets, as many times as you want without explaining yourself.

You can sit in solitude; drench yourself in the moon's distant gaze, grasp at the air, press it to palms, pray for an answer, without apologising.

You can start again as many times as you need to.

Because, each time you do, you will get better at hearing the ocean rising in your bones, the waves crashing against your chest, the warnings, the lessons, until the soft breeze of self-worth sweeps through your heart and you ascend.

We are always moving in the direction we think we deserve

Sometimes, you will spend your precious time walking straight back into the past; straight back into the pain and the guilt and the shame, because you truly believe that somewhere amongst the darkness you will find the answer.

But, you are here. So stay here. The answers will come once you untangle your body from the past and start walking upon the path carved out for you by the stars.

Women of the Earth

We make too many adjustments to try and preserve our identities whenever we find ourselves in situations that don't allow us to bloom in the way we deserve.

We must never forget that we deserve to bloom wherever we find ourselves.

The world does not need our silence. It needs our movement, our battle scars, worn with pride to show the next generation what resilience looks like.

The Earth's flowers

I am gathering the people who are rooted to growth;
whose intentions are as sweet as honeyed light.

Which is to say:

we are here to grow, to love, to spread,
without overshadowing each other.

It is our birthright to
stretch and grow towards the same
sun.

April Green

Everything is beautiful when you listen

Please try your hardest to accept what the Universe is giving you—don't try to control the force of life just because you need things to be as you want them to be.

Everything that is happening to you is happening for a reason.

(give yourself permission to believe this.)

You are allowed to start again

The past is part of you,
but it should never define
you.

Wherever you find
yourself,
start from there.

(your next step is aching with possibility.)

April Green

For the ones who have conquered fear, (and the ones walking behind them):

I think, when it all settles, and we watch the mountains—once too high, too heavy, too far away—crumbling into tiny fragments of dust; dissolving into air, we realise that we are stronger than we ever thought possible.

April Green

Say the hard things:
say the things
you are afraid to say,
because
letting them fall
from your mouth
like broken flowers
might just give another person
the courage to speak.

April Green

Inner dialogue

Measure your life upon your first thought of the day.

And if it isn't about your goal, the things you dream about for yourself, then close your eyes and start again.

April Green

She asked:

'What is grace?'

To which I replied:

'When you allow the sun to breathe
through your bones, the light to fall
from your eyes; then love:

you are grace.'

April Green

Becoming a Wildflower

If you happen to feel small:

Remember,
every day, there is more of you:

more footprints pressed upon the Earth
more heartbeats echoing through the air
more inhales filling your lungs
more memories lining your skin
more prayers resting between your fingers.

Yes—there is more of you than you ever thought
possible.

April Green

Becoming a Wildflower

The pain
of yesterday
will only leave you
when you step
fully
into today.

April Green

You are who you are

However you got here, whatever path you took, whatever storms you walked through, never regret the choices you made; because where you are now, is the result of those choices.

And every here, every now, is where your future starts.

I forgive myself:

for allowing others
to affect my sense
of worth.

Becoming a Wildflower

I forgive myself:

for shrinking to fit in,

for making mistakes,

for loving too hard,

for not loving hard enough,

for thinking that being different was anything other
than being unique,

for filling a hole in my soul with people and things
in the hope it would get smaller,

for crushing the pain inside my mouth like the blood
of a cherry only to spit out the truth and look for the
answer,

for chasing happiness between the sun rising and
the moon unstitching the day from my skin.

April Green

Forgiveness is for you

Forgive yourself for the mistakes you make while you are still growing, but please: learn from the mistakes you keep repeating. For it is bravely beautiful to openly meet your lessons; even when those lessons force you to delve into rough water.

I promise you will rise a better person.

Some souls
walk your path with you,

others,
a breath of air, a falling leaf.

In whatever form they arrive—
bless the Earth for guiding them
towards you.

Stand still

Stay connected to your own feelings: stay in your own energy, your own light. For if you allow yourself to be affected/hurt/shamed by the way another person feels about themselves, about you, about the world; then you are allowing your energy to intertwine with theirs—you are giving away your power.

The ones who try
to make you feel less,
are the ones least aware
of their own pain.

(be kind to them.)

I affirm:

to fall in love with myself—

> to hold all that I am
> with fragile, thankful hands

and know that I am holding a life,
a lesson, a future.

April Green

Becoming a Wildflower

Note to self:

I admire you
for recognising that certain
people and things
cause you pain.
For walking away.
For holding yourself together,
and apart,
at the same time.

But woman:

I admire you more
for never turning back.

April Green

For the ones struggling to move on:

The energy that brings closure to you
is not anger.

The energy that brings closure to you
is acceptance.

You are capable of everything you set your mind to

If you want to experience a life of freedom, then you have to choose the thoughts that break you away from the ones you have taught yourself to believe.

You have to find a way of living that doesn't pull your energy lower than the earth upon which you walk.

A life that keeps you grounded, but free to fly whenever you want.

The scent of love

Promise to never stop working
on yourself—
not so that others will like you more,
but because there is nothing sweeter
than waking up wrapped in the
knowledge
that you moulded every
part of who you are
from sunlight and storm;
and still have enough breath
inside you to whisper:

'I love myself.'

Poetry in motion

And once you make a deep connection with something like art, poetry, music, another soul—the air you breathe starts to carry more value.

Where you are isn't where you have already been

The most beautiful journey
starts where the light falls;
where you turn towards it,
catch it,
allow it to take you somewhere new.

(let the light teach you that you have a choice.)

April Green

The most important relationship

Self-love is a decision you make when you come to realise that everything you're experiencing is reflecting the relationship you have with yourself.

For the ones who are feeling unloved:

Your feelings,
like the weight of winter and thunder
and sunshine all at once,
are alive with all the things
that make the Universe alive.

Sweet human, don't allow the lonely days
to harden you.

You are here. And, if you can learn
how to be here, now;

then isn't that something like love?

A love note:

It's okay if you're not yet
where you want to be.

Remember:

You don't always notice
the sun rising in the sky
until, one day, you feel
its warmth touching your face
and you realise how much
you have grown.

Butterfly

Sometimes, you need to become
a different version of yourself before
your dream can manifest.

And that's okay.

You are allowed to let go
of the old you.

You are allowed to start again
as many times as you need to.

Hold onto faith,
no matter how heavy
it can sometimes feel in your arms;
hold onto it.

Because, faith is like making a promise
to yourself:

      things will get better soon.

The battle within

If the world seems out of balance—if all you can see is a storm clouding your view, then you must try to go within and untangle your inner conflicts. Because, I promise that nothing outside of yourself can ever resolve your own battles.

Never expect another person
to become the thing you need.

You have to find that
within yourself, first.

Don't destroy the good things

Look closely at how often you self-sabotage:

Question why you don't think you're worthy of what's falling onto your path; then find the part of you that's still in so much pain, so much discord, so much unrest.

For that part is crying out for acceptance and healing.

You cannot love and accept all that life
is giving you until you love and accept
all of yourself.

April Green

Life is for you; it's on your side

When life unfolds before you:
know that you don't have to change anything,

      you just have to be there, watching,
      breathing, moving forwards,

      arms wide open.

April Green

And when everything feels right:

       the reasons, the taste of the air, like
an answered prayer;

breathe it all in.

Because the right moments
can stay with you for a lifetime.

April Green

Love is attracted to the person who loves:

Some of us don't allow ourselves to experience the intrinsic nature of ourselves (love). We block it from flowing out of our hearts because we are afraid. But, the same life energy that empowers us to breathe, and think, and move, and sleep, is the very same energy that empowers us to love. It is the *fear* of love, (of who we are), that keeps the energy of love tucked inside our darkest corners.

Let love breathe.

Stop being afraid of the love inside you; stop holding back. Just keep giving, and giving, and giving with the undying faith that you can never be emptied of what you are made from.

Love is...

Love isn't only romantic. It's not the honey or the darling that you think you need in order to live a happy life.

Love is the friend who gives a voice to the words you desperately want to hear. Love is the person who says: 'it's not your fault; I know how you're feeling; I'm listening. Speak, shout, scream if you must; because soon, the tears will turn to laughter, and the pain will become a lesson for us both.'

When love is no longer
measured by butterflies
but by the soul's warmth
rising like the breeze of
a wing.

April Green

For the ones with low self-worth:

You are everything you see and beyond; but, too often, you're looking at life through the eyes of the past, the field of fear, the mistakes, the guilt, the pain and more.

So, I hope, maybe one day soon, you will learn to forgive yourself for carrying such a heavy, blinding weight, and you will find the courage to open your eyes a little wider and start afresh.

You are perfect as you are.
Keep growing, but don't ever change
your inherent nature.

Fall,
as many times as it takes;
because you will always rise
with the nectar of flowers
in your hair
and some kind of sweet faith
in your bones.

(you will always rise stronger.)

April Green

The taste of rain

When it rains, I still tilt my face to the sky in honour of the girl who once forgot that those water-light kisses from heaven are sent to remind us to absorb every atom of life.

To be mercy
and compassion
and unconditional
acceptance

all at once.

I believe very deeply
in the power you have
to build yourself back up.

You are your own light:

        you do not need anyone else
to shine for you.

April Green

For the ones struggling to understand themselves:

The parts you are hiding from yourself;
the parts that are echoing through your bones
like the dust of dancing stars—

these are the magic parts.

A love note

Choose what matters most to you
and nurture it.

If it is peace,
then find a way to bring peace
into your life; (find a way to fight less
with yourself.)
If it is a dream,
then start by taking one step
towards its creation.
If it is a relationship,
then start with the one you have
with yourself.

Be patient with yourself. Be kind to yourself.

(no-one hurts us more than we hurt ourselves.)

Today:
you are allowed to breathe
the colour of sunflowers and
start again.

April Green

And above all,
I hope the scent of earth
never leaves your skin.

(stay grounded.)

I am afraid.
But the sky in the distance
looks something like faith,
so I will keep walking.

— acknowledgements —

sasha, tina, xavier

&
a very special thank-you to my readers.

your love and support means more to me than you
will ever know.

love,
april green

Instagram and twitter: @loveaprilgreen